# Embers in the House of Night

Selected Poems of
## Edvard Kocbek

Translated from the Slovene by
Sonja Kravanja

With an Introduction by
Richard Jackson

This translation is dedicated to Steven Schwartz and the Board of Directors of the Witter Bynner Foundation for Poetry. Their continuous support and appreciation of poetry-in-translation is invaluable.

Support for the publication of this volume was also granted by The Trubar Foundation, Association of Slovenian Writers.

Lumen, Inc.
3900 Paseo del Sol
Santa Fe, New Mexico 87505
www.lumenbooks.org
ISBN: 0-930829-42-5
Printed in the United States of America
*Embers in the House of Night* © 1999 Lumen, Inc.
Translation © 1999 Sonja Kravanja
Poems in this collection were selected by Sonja Kravanja from Edvard Kocbek's
*Zbrane pesmi 1* and *2* 1977 © Matjaz Kocbek
Distributed by Consortium Book Sales & Distribution
1-800-283-3572

# Contents

## Translator's Preface

It is not that I didn't know this before, but it just struck me for the first time with its full force: here I am at the annual ALTA conference in Guadalajara, in a city of six million people, reading poetry from Slovenia, a nation of two million people. The Slovene language in Guadalajara? Then Octavio Paz comes to mind—his "Labyrinth of Solitude: Life and Thought in Mexico" in particular—and I think of Edvard Kocbek. Without consciously comparing the two, it comes to me as an epiphany—Edvard Kocbek was for the Slovenes what Octavio Paz was for the Mexicans: not only a man of profound seriousness and reflection, but also a writer who never compromised—not in his poems, not in his essays, not in his life, a man who was the spiritual and intellectual father of his nation's thought and culture.

But, while Paz was long honored, both in his own country and internationally, Kocbek gained recognition only a few years before his death in 1981. For fifteen years before that he lived in virtual isolation, banned from both public life and publishing. In other words, Kocbek was shunned by his own people (read: government) for political reasons, and because of the freedom of his thought—it was his thought they had to put under arrest. And while they could confine him, he nevertheless remained morally unfettered, unshattered; he never compromised, he continued to write and translate with an unabated passion, dignity and composure. This integrity drew me to him: the depth of his thought, the essential human issues revealed in his writings, the primeval emotions evoked.

This is my personal anthology. The title for the book came to me only after I finished both the selection and translation. I did not attempt, nor had I any ambition to translate only poems that are the most known or thought to be his best. Rather I translated those poems that captivated me, stirred in me an emotion, revealed a truth, made me pause with their delicate imagistic power—in short, engaged me fully as a human being and as a translator.

I never met Edvard Kocbek. And yet, by re-creating his poems in another language, I encountered him on the deepest of levels. With a soul enriched, understandings deepened—I can call this encounter nothing but an honor.

Sonja Kravanja
Guadalajara, Mexico, December 1998

# Remaking the Lexicon:
## The Relevance of Edvard Kocbek Today

Richard Jackson

Language comes first. Obviously, it is what a poem is made out of, as opposed to musical or visual representations in other arts. Sir Philip Sydney called it *energia*, which he derived from Longinus's sense of the poem as creating linguistic excitement. Energy provides a sense of mystery without being merely confusing. The contemporary poet Charles Simic, an admirer of Kocbek, says: "Poetry is an orphan of silence. . . . Occasionally people think of silence as of something negative, passive. For me, silence is spiritual energy." Language is not only what is spoken but what is unspoken. The unspoken is the mystery, but it is also part of the spoken in an odd sense. The relationship between the spoken and the unspoken gives a sense of texture. Heidegger writes: "Only where there is language is there world, i.e, the perpetually altering circuit of decision and production, of action and responsibility, but also of commotion and arbitrariness, of decay and confusion." In other words, language is what moves us from a placid and general-ized view of the world, the world of the reductive, to a world of complex, variable, interesting responses—to the human, to the poetry of Kocbek, the great Slovene poet, philosopher, religious thinker, and dissident who died in 1981 at the age of 77:

*I am unable to sleep,*
*a big disaster*
*surrounds me,*
*words that I have spoken*
*and sent out into the world*
*are suddenly returning weary,*
*ill, dreadfully anxious,*
*they seek a refuge from destruction . . .*

So begins Kocbek's poem "Death of Words," written at a time when perhaps the first tremors of the current crisis in central and eastern Europe could be felt by someone with enough sensitivity and vision. He goes on to list all the usual categories of failed feeling and thinking, of failed language, but at the end, in the midst of despair, begins to glimpse a solution:

*I am unable to stretch my arm,*
*or open my mouth,*
*am unable to caress the word despair or*
*say anything to the words solace, deliverance,*
*the words toy and grace are choking me,*
*on my eyes land those shot as they fled,*
*man, mother, love, loyalty,*
*the unhappy ones I neglected or never uttered*
*settle on my chest*
*but one of them has nestled*
*right between my trembling lips,*
*never have I seen it in the lexicon.*

Which is this neglected one? What word perhaps may have fared better? In a fragmented world where no universals bind together common assumptions, hopes and values, could any words have fared better? And yet this is a word not even in the lexicon that he refers to at the end; it is a word beyond words, what all poetry aspires to. For Kocbek it seems we must escape all the previous categories held in our language or they will come back, misunderstood, mistreated, misinterpreted by an increasingly fragmented world, to haunt us. It is a question, then, of forging identities beyond the self, and therefore identities that are not going to be exclusive, but inclusive. It is a task our very language and symbol system seems, as Kocbek suggests, unable to deal with, but a task that we, as writers, must confront.

What Kocbek confronts in his art are all the forces that lie beyond us, that threaten us, that destabilize the world our language creates. They may be forces of ethnic identity or military force or government bureaucracy, even the power of rhetoric itself. In the end, even the self's identity is threatened when language becomes unstable. And yet the poet himself must destabilize language in order to renew it. The problem for a poet like Kocbek, then, becomes an ethical one. The poem itself must question its own procedures and perspectives—sometimes by shifting stylistic gears, posing hypotheses, suggesting alternatives, changing tone or course in the middle, keeping an ironic tone. The technique of a Kocbek poem often calls itself into question in order to widen the range of its possibilities. Kocbek's poems have nothing of the ideological and rigid about them precisely for this reason. Their irony creates a richness of experience that is manifest in the ability of the poet, like Keats or Stevens, to turn a potentially bleak vision into a triumphant one. And these turns in Kocbek's poems create an opportunity for the poet, and for the reader, to experience the very process of creating another, healthier, more hopeful world.

It is all the more remarkable for a writer in our own age to be able to maintain such an art—no easy task for the writer, to be sure. Today, with so many fissures based upon ethnic, historical, political, religious and other differences that seem ready to separate us, poets often resort to propaganda or simplistic world views. Kocbek does not simply report on a world, he changes it; the responsibility of the artist to suggest something beyond our own limits is perhaps the driving force of his work. Here is the poem "In The Torched Village:"

*I lean on the wall,*
*still hot*
*from a long fire,*
*no villagers,*
*no foe around,*
*the ground gives way,*
*the universe crumbles,*
*the stars perish.*

*A sudden ripple*
*of the scent of violets.*
*I begin to listen*
*to tender voices,*
*the grass raising*
*for new footsteps,*
*the ashes embracing*
*a new solidity.*

*A brook clatters*
*into a stone trough,*
*a cat returns*
*to a scorched doorstep.*
*I grow larger,*
*become a giant,*

*now I see over*
*the shoulder of all horror.*

The movement here enacts a reversal of positions and perspectives that is essential. The defeated man leaning against the charred wall at the beginning of the poem, dwarfed by the "universe" that is falling apart and the dying "stars," becomes, by the end of the poem, the colossus for whom these tragedies of war, personified by "horror," are themselves dwarfed by his encompassing vision. It is a vision, as the middle of the poem asserts, that comes not from huge political statements or poems, but tiny observations, the loving perspective of "tender voices." Perhaps the turnabout comes most subtly in the sense that "the ashes embrace a new solidity," the very images of desolation from earlier in the poem made here to enact a new beginning. What the poem does, what the writer can do, is suggest ways to transform our language of death into a language of life. Of course, the practical and accepted view about all this would be to say that nothing can be done, that changing the language or changing the vision is scant help, but to do so would be simply to maintain a sort of planned or programmed refusal to feel. If we are to look for identities in cultures and in literatures, we must go beyond the unique, but finally transitory items that constitute a specific culture and a specific culture's history; we must find the "never uttered" words of Kocbek that tie us all together. Otherwise our cultures eventually become armed camps. Otherwise our words will come back, dead or dying. Otherwise we will find that we contain only meteoric fragments of a world long exploded at its most basic and essential level, the atom.

      All of which is to say that Kocbek is a poet essential for our difficult times, to paraphrase Hölderlin. In some ways he harks back to the great Romantics, such as Keats, especially through the eyes of the Slovene Romantic poet, Preseren; in other ways he harks back to the great visionary questing poets, such as Shelley in "Alastor," and further back, especially, to Dante and Petrarch, especially in the way they idealize that unspoken language in the form of an ideal that the poet seeks. This is perhaps most evident if we think of Kocbek's relation to women in the context of Dante's Beatrice and Petrarch's Laura, even the Biblical Song of Songs: what they all have in common is a way of idealizing the ineffable in a feminine mode. There is a mystical quality to the unuttered.

Take, for example, the poem "Divine Search." Here the poet-speaker searches for a beautiful maiden and seems to float across waves, clouds, whatever elements hold the universe together. As the quest goes on, all that is "sinful and alien" seems to fall away and he seems to have the power to float across waves and clouds, the cosmos, as a spiritual being. And yet for all that he is afraid he will encounter the "terrifying nothingness"—a more intense version of what we saw in "[title]"—for he is aware that "something essential is fleeing." So the poet searches for the ineffable, an ideal, aware that he may find that there is none, only a nothingness, and yet it is the image and substance of woman per se that gives a quiet, mature strength. In the end, he understands himself as "wanderer, wizard and lover" in all sense of those words, fully ironic and so fully recognizing their possibilities.

These wonderful translations by Sonja Kravanja represent a major accomplishment, for they very subtly draw out both the music and complexity of Kocbek's poems, which are at once formal and also allow an idiomatic tone and atmosphere. These are, among the various translations available, the best. A good deal of the effect of these poems comes from their sense of pacing and timing—hard things for any translator to gather, but Kravanja has provided a wonderfully accurate rendering of these effects. These translations remind us not of Frost's notion that poetry is what is lost in translation, but Brodsky's larger sense that poety is what is gained in translation.

September 1998
Chattanooga, Tennessee

## THE LIPPIZANERS

A newspaper reports:
the Lippizaners collaborated
on a historical film.
A radio explains:
a millionaire had bought the Lippizaners,
the noble animals were quiet
throughout the journey over the Atlantic.
And a text book teaches:
the Lippizaners are graceful riding horses,
their origin is in the Karst, they are of supple hoof,
conceited trot, intelligent nature,
and obstinate fidelity.

But I have to add, my son,
that it isn't possible to fit these
restless animals into any set pattern:
it is good, when the day shines,
the Lippizaners are black foals.
And it is good, when the night reigns,
the Lippizaners are white mares,
but the best is,
when the day comes out of the night,
then the Lippizaners are the white and black buffoons,
the court fools of its Majesty,
Slovenian history.

Others have worshipped holy cows and dragons,
thousand-year-old turtles and winged lions,
unicorns, double-headed eagles and phoenixes,
but we've chosen the most beautiful animal,

which proved to be excellent on battlefields, in circuses,
harnessed to princesses and the Golden Monstrance,
therefore the emperors of Vienna spoke
French with skillful diplomats,
Italian with charming actresses,
Spanish with the infinite God,
and German with uneducated servants:
but with the horses they talked Slovene.

Remember, my child, how mysteriously
nature and history are bound together,
and how different are the driving forces of the spirit
of each of the world's peoples.
You know well that ours is the land of contests and races.
You, thus, understand why the white horses
from Noah's ark found a refuge on our pure ground,
why they became our holy animal,
why they entered into the legend of history,
and why they bring the life pulse to our future.
They incessantly search for our promised land
and are becoming our spirit's passionate saddle.

I endlessly sit on a black and white horse,
my beloved son,
like a Bedouin chief
I blend with my animal,
I've been traveling on it all my life,
I sleep on it, and I dream on it,
and I'll die on it.
I learned all our prophesies
on the mysterious animal,

and this poem, too, I experienced
on its trembling back.

Nothing is darker than
clear speech,
and nothing more true than a poem
the intellect cannot seize,
heroes limp in the bright sun,
and sages stammer in the dark,
the buffoons, though, are changing into poets,
the winged Pegasi run faster and faster
above the caves of our old earth
jumping and pounding—
the impatient Slovenian animals
are still trying to awaken the legendary King Matjaz.

Those who don't know how to ride a horse,
should learn quickly
how to tame the fiery animal,
how to ride freely in a light saddle,
how to catch the harmony of the trot,
and above all to persist in the premonition,
for our horses came galloping from far away,
and they still have far to go:
motors tend to break down,
elephants eat too much,
our road is a long one,
and it is too far to walk.

## LANDSCAPE

The spirits of wild animals
approach houses
pregnant women
move their lips;
these ripened spaces smell
of greasy matter
and rumbling wheat.
Fruit has fed the worms,
flowers returned
to their nocturnal beehive,
the landscape retreats
behind its image.
Silence rattles its ancient sound,
memory weighs the anchor,
moonlight toys
with the peacock's tail.
Things grow larger
than their presence,
drunks can't get their fill of thirst
or animals to the bottom
of their innocence.
The wind feeds on abysses,
darkness on thieves.
The world is riddled
with longing pains,
I spin within the magic circle
as in nuptial dreams
unable to recall
the redemptive incantation.

# EMBER

A distant window is lit, hollow,
the red light flickering as if
someone wished to snuff it out,
but it fights back
with an unabated resilience.
At times it darkens,
at times it glows,
scorching me with heat,
it is you.

I wither flapping,
my fire burned down to embers,
now the wind blows over its charred cinders
poking at it at times;
smoldering embers flash hot,
flicker, and then, tamed, wink out.
Breathing imperceptibly,
my utterly spent heart
still obeys me,
panting slowly.

My physical self is burned to the ground
and only glimmers in the soil
crushed into a magnificent alloy.
I move ardently, tremulous and transitory,
through fissures,
through green and red and sky blue,
through the terrifying window of colors
above which lingers a tender dawn.

Never was I
such a beautiful volcano.

## MYSTERY WOMAN

Unforgettable miracle in the garden of Eden,
the changeable image of Vida-the-Beautiful,
the unraveled fairy-tale in Sanskrit,
the wind of Atlantis in the sails of dreamtime.

You hurry down the streets of the world, the opium
of changes, ecstasies, and magics of palimpsest,
the forever mysterious beautiful lady,
you are the start of my sorrowful story.

At times the sweet oblivion of the angel's wings,
the eternal glory of a celestial lover;
at times the empty horror of sinful lust,
the temptation redeemed by a magnificent force.

You: the wounded wilds of Diana.
I: the golden sword of a fairy tale prince.
You are snow falling silently on the hot palm
of my hand and disappearing in an instant.

Edvard Kocbek

## REQUEST

I implore my memory to reach back, to seize all doubts
and despairs, all hopes and passions, all dreams and funerals,
all prophecies and disappointments, all the killed, crippled
and wounded, desecrated, all exalted on altars and wrapped in
flags, all intoxicated by happiness and sobered from sorrow, let me
remember all weepings and jubilations, all funny stories and loves,
all sins, all leaps into the unknown, all fires, floods, earthquakes
and God's commandments, let all the tender fragile ties that bind
body and soul, me and someone else, be revealed, let me perceive
all conceptions and gentle abandons, all the shameful
confessions and states of purity, let the remembrances of all
these vibrate inside me and my surroundings, and let me be
included in the collective guilt and the collective absolution.
I, thus, request to be able to keep neighbors in front of and behind
me, be the middleman of messages from the future even though
they at times are strange, incomprehensible, threatening or
calming, brief or tedious. It is probable that none of us fully
understands the whole game, but courage itself is absolute
and all-knowing.

## TRAFFIC LIGHT

Rushing river with wild rafts
a red sign hovers
we gaze at it
on the opposite bank other hunters
pant from the same persecution
we stare at one another's bellies and pockets
rage flares up on both sides
such is the law of these parts:
who will get whom.

An irrepressible suspicion is stirred
an insane greed of few moments
a lesson in anatomy, dress-rehearsal of bandits
the first spontaneous revolution
we touch hips, chests, and secrets
phantoms and apparitions hustle together
with other mirages, gasping
gold, scents, prison orders
in a few moments I am both drunk and sober.

The sign is red, the ground quaking
silence hoarse, speech abdominal
arms dragging the ground like an orangutan's
inscriptions crazy, restaurants become raids
my letter has no commas or periods
the eviction from paradise continues
the Gordian knot chokes my throat
I will slip on snake's saliva
seek restlessly the chiefs of protocol;
a green sign appears.

No one can hold us back any longer
each needs to reach the bottom of his passions:
the one who carries the body of a savior
the one who is driven in a red cart
the one who sneaks away with stolen money
the one who fragments instead of the state
the one who spreads the alphabet-sect teachings
the one who performs abortions
the one whose teeth are made of the bishop's ring
and the one who will have to die twice.

## GIFT OF A POEM

Since time immemorial poets have been asked
to capture, like solemn historians,
with precise language,
events in human history worth preserving
so that the old and the young
would learn them by heart and sing their sadness,
their glory, their lessons for generations to come.
And, behold, poets have always let their spirits soar
and connected their holy duty to history
with an irrepressible passion for the primal game.
They wrote poems of how rain and snow
fulfill their duties in nature,
how a diligent farmer sows
his plowed fields in fall and reaps them in summer.
A distinctive graciousness permeates me now.
It is inspired by everything that
mankind has forever held in honor,
it surpasses my memory, coupling with all
that breathes with the universe and imagination.
I feel now more than ever that
a poem is the condensed force of all man's
talents and its power lies
in transcending language.

Edvard Kocbek

## HISTORY

History, the blind tumult of man,
the incessant conflict of good and evil,
the sinking of infernal noise into a bottomless pit,
one solemn confusion from morning till night,
the victory shouts of conquerors and the wailing of the defeated,
history, the drilling of memory and the sweetness
of oblivion, banners in the wind, clattering of drums,
stampede of horses, the astonishment of slaughtered
guards, pretenders and informers, technological
discoveries and dreams of Babylon, the merry-go-round
of fame with short rests in between for the new
onslaught, attacks and withdrawals, building and destruction,
crawling in the dark and smoldering under ashes
cradles and warplanes, tanks and bridal
wreaths, history, where are your ecstasies
and manifests, where are you golden
wreaths and marble monuments, where are your
prophecies and hidden loves, what are your intentions,
you, so-called leaders
of mankind, what is hidden in your whispers behind dark glasses,
what is the meaning of your silence
of your loquacity, of your continuous meetings
and secret talks, pilgrims knock in vain
on other doors, artists connect in vain arches
of palaces rising from new foundations, in vain children write
slogans on the walls, in vain are the discoveries in megaphones
in vain the sacrificing of womankind, in vain
parades and volleys, volleys as greetings, volleys
as warnings, volleys for punishment, too many
bans, too many orders, as if there were
no sky, as if there were no man.

## PARROTS

Termites attacked the land,
hollowed out bridges and monuments,
even tables and beds crumbled to dust.
Germs invaded laboratories,
settled on the sterilized instruments,
fooling learned men in the process.
It all happened in a terrifying silence.

In our case it was a plague of parrots
—green and yellow—they screeched
in gardens, our houses, and kitchens.
Ravenous, filthy and vulgar
they invaded our bathrooms and bedrooms
and finally settled inside people.
It all happened with a terrifying noise.

None of us knows how to lie anymore,
and none can tell the truth;
we speak the tongue of an unknown tribe,
we yell and curse, howl and wail,
widen our mouths, and strain our eyes;
even the court jester has gone insane
and is screeching like all the rest.

Somewhere, though, stands a circle of men
gazing mutely at the still center;
motionless they stand in blessed silence,
their shoulders growing broader
under its ancient burden.
When they suddenly turn around
the parrots in us will die.

## MAN ALIVE NEXT TO A DEAD ONE

Who built the magnificent statues
on Easter Island?
What tell the hidden manuscripts
in Tibetan caves?
What knowledge reveal the explorations of Peru?
Who is whispering under Mt. Spik?
All parts of the earth are of genius.
Each mountain screams in thunderstorms.
Each lake despairs in fog.
Plains crawl at night
arriving nowhere.
But they are there waiting for us.
It is better to be a tamed beast
than an angry animal.
I cannot imagine a man anywhere
whose ruffled hairy skin
has never been caressed by anyone.
Not even acupuncture helps him
any longer, some stars die
young, some are sadly aging.
Therefore I suggest kneeling on ashes and caress
the innocent shadow placed in dreams.
Some wondrous occurrences happen at the time of death.
When Stalin died
the mass of people at his funeral
was so concentrated that, in the freezing cold,
there rose from its terror and breath
a white cloud.

## HOMELY WOMAN

Look at the homely woman stooped over the soil,
her heart beats fast, she gasps as
she passes us.

No one returns her greeting. When she disappears
beyond the brook we stop dead like captives, our
hearts constrict, steps grow heavy.

Our dying will be strange, we've lost something invaluable.
The homely woman's candle burns incessantly, filling
the evening church with profound silence.

## MAIDEN'S APRON

When she paused on the hilltop
and turned toward my warm wind
she dropped her apron out of fear;
it was full of old huts and trees
that rolled down the slope
and formed themselves into an ineffable village.
I strode into the nearest sanctuary
and pierced the wall of its accumulated memory;
the scents and fragrances inebriated me,
the magic overpowered me, making me
insane for half of eternity.
I woke up very late
and leaned against the wind—
it was still warm—
and slowly started to fill up her apron
with houses, courtyards, barns,
hay and moonlight, sighs and laughter.
The church bell I lay in with the utmost care
so it would not chime too loud.

## AMONG GRASSES

You can no longer lean and lie down
heavy, intoxicated, among grasses.
Over the warm soil hovers a tall night,
you are hardly visible
in the dark breathing of young blades.

I receive you humbly, sweet lady,
I fall on my knees, loyal to the wild.
My hands have found your closed eyes:
O insane sadness of distant fires,
O quiet harmony of miracles in the dark.

## GOOD PREMONITION

I climbed the foothill
of the day
as if searching
a construction site
for a cathedral.
When I reached
a solitary clearing
I stopped;
it was as tranquil
as the happy nest
of a wren.
I closed my eyes,
bent my head,
and whispered:
it is true, my lady friend,
that I should lie here
two feet underground,
at peace with myself and transformed
like a bay at nightfall
or the gold on an icon.
I'd fall asleep here,
next to you,
creating dew with the sun,
nourishing grass and the wind
carrying the love songs of quails
and the scurrying of rabbits.
It is here I'd be able to
reach the ultimate peace,
I, the enlightened dreamer,
the Indian boy,

under the fan of dawns
and rituals of the sun
on the eyelashes of darkness.
I'd glow with fireflies,
swing with the stars,
sob with secret lovers,
returning time and again
to the fiery land.

## ANOTHER ABYSS TO CROSS

What a beautiful, sunny, tranquil day;
no pressures, horrors,
acquaintances or spies.
Bursting with health I am aching from the beauty
of exquisite bodies and kind faces
that draw me back to paganism, fetishism
and ancient myths evoked from
the waiting substance of every beautiful being.
But at nightfall an ineffable memory
quietly stalks me, I resist it,
waiting for the conflict
and finally, I carry myself
as a horse does the wounded.
The people around me are proud of their fears,
talking about their minor wounds,
but nobody notices my open side.
I bleed all night, writing on walls
with my own blood the ancient story of my origin,
while their tales fill the pages of books.
There is nothing on earth more devastating than a woman
you make love to one night only,
and can never find again.

## MOUNTAIN

Whenever I look at you, you are magnificent
and when I gaze at your peak from nearby
my lips start to tremble, whispering, oh sacred
mountain, oh solemn and mysterious mountain, oh
untamed and maternal mountain, oh
the primal and bold flight toward the sky,
full of sighs and venerable memories,
oh dreaming mountain, locked within yourself,
bearing myriads of scars. You seem indifferent
to your secrecy, but in truth your serenity
terrifies me, though I can never see you from all sides.
In silence I hear the purity of your memories,
sense your eternal walk toward home,
and knowing you'll reach it,
your calm assurance is ancient.
You force a man who looks upon you
to doubt himself, discovering your
true secret: you are the most magnificent pregnant woman,
shyly close to giving birth,
shifting imperceptibly in choosing the beautiful green dress
with white and blue flowers,
you are on your way to the secret place
the volcanic breath has awakened in you.
Your breathing agitates the wild animals and tells
of the widening of your womb,
your breasts are swelling from divine milk
and wild honey,
the clouds above you tell the story
of your indestructible mythology,
they all want to be part of the celebration

of you giving birth
and I, too, am in awe, am repeating
the words of glory: oh magnificent mountain,
oh wild mountain, oh sacred and solemn mountain,
the maternal, the mysterious.

## CHURCH IN THE SLOVENIAN HILLS

Dappled tent
of weary pilgrims
the protective color
of the wise turtle
lichen of ancient nights
moss of placid forests
the silence of a butterfly—
duration achieved by
patience—
but it is not a sphinx
or a fish
or a fairy dragon
but a weary ox
with a thick head
leaning against the sky
opening at times
his kind eyes
for the fragrant hay
and the intoxicated incense
for a cock in the wind
and bronze bells
he still watches over
the holy manger
connecting existent things
with those not yet created;
there are no cracks
be still, heart
beat softly
so that the message
of the silent parchment
does not fall
to dust.

## STANDING BY A VESSEL

I stand by a jug, unable to pass by.
My spirit, caught in a game,
bends over the vessel of
quenched thirst. I drank out of it
in the strongly scented hay of the meadow, lovely
king's daughters carried it to a spring,
and an unknown painter placed a blossom
of the heart into it.

Precious vessel, let me see you in your
glory: enveloped in the afternoon silence
you stand firm, staring tranquil,
with wide-open eyes,
into uncertainty.

## BLACK SEA

All our waters
gravitate toward you,
Black Sea.
The dew of mornings,
evening thunderstorms
and all the springs
murmur into you,
Tatar Sea.
Snows, avalanches
and floods
hasten to meet you,
Turkish Sea.
With them our
fragile soil is torn away,
dropping together with
sacred ashes
onto your bottom,
Byzantine Sea.
Together with our soil
our bodies
sink into you,
the merciless sea.
We already are in your algae
and your ravenous fish,
we have become a part of your depth,
Black Sea.

## PONTUS

Where I am now is the Pontus.
The Pontus is exile.
Exile is reminiscent of paradise,
though paradise I cannot remember.
My enemy's power has faded,
it no longer confronts me with fervor,
no longer returns me to myself.

I walk over fields and mountains,
open books and watch birds,
searching for my opponent.
I call to it and long for it
to rouse me vehemently.
But: exile is freedom
with no opponent,
no confrontation.

## MICROPHONE IN THE WALL

We are finally alone
you and I,
but don't even think
of taking it easy or resting
for your work is just now starting.
You will listen to my silence
which is loquacious
and draws you to the depth of truth.
Listen carefully now,
you beast with no eyes or tongue,
monster with ears only.
My spirit talks without voice,
shouts and screams inaudibly
with joy to have you here,
you Great Suspicion,
hungering for me to reveal myself.
My silence is opening books
and dangerous manuscripts,
lexicons and prophets,
ancient truths and laws,
stories of loyalty and torture.
There is no way you can rest,
you have to swallow this, gulp it down
though you are already choking
and your ear is exhausted.
You are unable to interrupt me
or say anything in return;
my time has arrived
and I insult you, curse you,
you impostor, poisoner,

desecrator, slave, satan,
machine, death, death.
You swallow your shame
and are condemned to listen
not to speak,
because you are a monster
with only ears
and a bellyful of treason;
no tongue or truth,
you are helpless, can call me neither weakling
nor powerful,
cannot utter words like "grace" or "despair,"
shout to me to stop
though you are burning with slavish rage.
I greet you, crippled creature,
am glad you are here
immured day and night,
you cursed extension of the Great Suspicion,
the diabolical belly of inhuman force
which is so feeble that it shudders day and night.
Now you evoke my power
my unified an undivided power,
I cannot plant someone else
in my place
I am who I am—
restlessness and searching,
sincerity and pain,
faith, hope, love,
your magnificent counter-suspicion—
you never can divide me,
make me your double,
catch me

lying or calculating.
You'll never be the executioner of my conscience,
you don't have a choice
but to swallow my joy
or, at times, my sadness.
You, my enemy,
my infertile neighbor
so different and inhuman
unable to break loose
to become insane or to commit suicide.
I can tell
I wore you out,
your tail is between your legs
but this is only an outline
of my revenge:
my true revenge
is a poem.
You will never know me,
your ears have no light,
will be hushed by the passage of time
while I am a tongue-flame
fire
that will never cease to burn
and scorch.

NOW

When I spoke
they said I was mute;
when I wrote
they said I was blind;
when I left them
they said I was lame.
When they were calling me back
they found out I was deaf.
They turned my senses upside down
and came to the conclusion I was crazy.
Now I am happy.

IN PRAISE OF DEATH

I cherish you, my friend, who thinks of me incessantly,
  waiting for me calm and serene, with your arm leaning
  on the edge of evening.
My beloved, I hear the rustling of your duration as summer
  shifts into fall, winter into spring, you participate
  in the suffering of matter, gaze through the world's
  transparency.
You are my encounter on the doorstep, an image between walls,
  an invocation in the volume of space, a rite of sacrifice
  in the motionless.
You send wind to me and I wither, you chime in the sun and
  I become a bee, in silence you offer your composed
   mouth
  to me and I change like a childbearing woman.
You toyed with me in my shepherd's days, tearing our
  kites apart, breaking vessels, dreamily bewitching us
  with colored glass.
On each day something shattered, in each night there was
  the presence of your dark blossom.
You left a longing color in my sleepy eyes, you darkened
  all my visibility, solitary inebriation became
  my peacock's tail.
Now I am like a dove on the doorstep of a sanctuary, like
  a maiden from faraway islands being taken to a sacrificial
  fire.
All that exists is an arch of people bidding farewell, I bend
  my head under the weight of each moment, close my eyes
  from opiate obligation.
My eyelashes pulse like the fluttering of a dark bird, light
  and darkness are your loyal guardians.

Slowly you suck me into yourself, I feel sweet pain as I turn
        toward a different side of the sky, pluck a fruit, or
        tear my glance away from a woman.
You anchor deeper and deeper in me, my body is shrinking, and
        I treasure my longing to serve the supreme.
I greet you, my friend, you place an animal on silent grass,
        and strip away its seeds; you close man's eyes and he
        sinks into a fathomless sleep.

## PEOPLE AND ANIMALS IN MUD

People and animals in the mud, the last grasses
by the ditches filled with turbid waters, the enamored
hurry in the dark, fissures rustle in the deep,
calling, calling.

Trees have remained alone, dull insects
languish, the gray sky resembles a corpse, the forlorn
lamp burns, O womb of memory's horrors,
calling, calling.

We are returning not knowing when we'll
return, rain clatters, waters gather, darkness
saturates the world, place your hand in mine, the heart chimes,
calling, calling.

## TRANSFORMATION

Raging space suddenly calmed down
and powerful time grew silent
people fell on their knees
struck dumb by the depths
of atrocious wrath
the future glory permeated them
a gentle breeze began to blow
they quivered from bread and wine
someone uttered words
"this is my body
this is my blood"
the glowing truth of the day
three four moments of an earthquake
the bowels of earth shift
mountains grasp the sky
the ocean bottom sighs with relief
trees hasten their growth
neighboring houses hug each other
men are conceiving with fury
and women giving birth with shouting
the children, though, write an essay;
Why I am not bored.

## SENTENCE

Not this earth I grow from
and caress its shadow
not this earth, but the other
where nothing opened can be closed
where no longer exist the outside inside
or the inside outside
where multi-eyed sides of the world
play with insane inventions
where objects unbutton their breasts
and it is all made of mother's milk
and father's storytelling
where you can no longer broaden anything
or make peculiar mistakes
where being relieved comes easy
and you play with naught because of its depth
where you grow but never catch up with yourself
and everything finished is prepared for the new
ah, that other land
where a stag's antler
already is the whole stag,
that other land will be my ruin.

## SCENT OF A WOMAN

The primordial time seems so far away
and yet so mercilessly close.
Some days are painfully pure
and people so dark
I wonder how I can breathe at all,
how my lungs expand and
how dangerously, relentlessly,
I live my life, wild at heart.
Only when a noble hunger for the smell
of a woman awakens in me
does the life of my body become
high and deep, wide
and so virginal I can feel my soul
and everything I am composed of,
but above all
I remember my time in the cradle
where the sweet smell of a woman
is the most painful and the most intoxicating.
Then I unwillingly lean forward
as if this sweetness will draw me down to earth
from which I will never rise again.

CLIMAX

The night's lens widens
consuming the earth and the stars,
lifting the two of us
to the fiery sky
where we flame up, a gigantic torch.

But as you open the depth
of your eyes,
your power becomes stronger than the night's;
you embrace space and time,
games of the raving universe,
ecstasies, catastrophes, laws,
the whole seven eons of creation.

Only then you awaken me,
I broaden my eyes' pupils,
lean over your game,
drink the eternity of your eyes,
battle the horror of finality through the night
until I can master your love
and become the giant among giants,
the solitary man.

Edvard Kocbek

## STRANGE OCCURRENCE

Repetition of a phenomenon:
a twitching I am unable to control.
At times uniform crackling.
As if from wood drying in rooms.
At day and at night the easing of tension
now in furniture, then in the floor,
somewhere in the wall, in the lamp-post, between books.
Always someplace else and always inevitable—
like before an earthquake, or
as if a treacherous force were accumulating,
the house about to crush, or an immured man
poised to knock on the wall and step out of it
any time. I swallow hard as I become
a captive of this crackle. The senses are sharp
and I know: the warm silence of objects,
the horrifying aloneness of ancient and bored matter.
It will rebel, sooner or later. Even now the ocean
is sweeping over England. Even now the glowing magma
is collapsing under our feet. In the dark I read
an unkown writing on the walls. In the dark I see huge eyes,
and in dreams the raging of primeval storms.

## DARK IMAGE

Since you've invaded us you keep stirring us up,
thrust in our veins, glow in our eyes, pull at our hearts;
you blow up bodies, destroy worlds, O red blood,
always warm and greasy, O you sweet cider
of the ancient and wild autumn.

O holy human blood, we drank you out of hands
and golden chalices, we mixed you with wine
and dipped our banners into you. You dripped down
the dictators' beards and out of a princess's
fine finger in fairy tales.

The whole earth is sprinkled with you,
you ran into sand, colored rocks red, wetted grass
and nourished fish. You erupted out of mouths
and hips, trickled down in silent stripes,
flooding our eyes.

The sticky earth can no longer see, the dead lie immovable,
our blood emits no scent. Be loyal, my fathomless heart,
holler and scream after the lost horror,
the cheated heart, as dangerous as a madman.

## CRUCIFIX IN A FIELD

When, on Corpus Christi day,
an altar was placed beneath him
some saw his eyes open slowly,
his narrow nostrils widen
blissful from incense.

Fragrances followed,
scents of wheat and grasses, fog,
smoke of fires, acrid gunpowder;
a mysterious shot pierced his brow,
and his head, laden with thorns
and hay blades, bowed heavily.
He lost human likeness,
became a scarecrow.

Raging forces were unleashed
lusting for horror.
He now hangs on one nail only
and, some night when the wind
leaps with an immense veneration,
he will suddenly break free,
step on the safe ground
and kiss it.

## IN A TORCHED VILLAGE

I lean on the wall
still hot
from a long fire,
no villagers
no foe around,
the ground gives way,
the universe crumbles,
the stars perish.

A sudden ripple
of the scent of violets.
I begin to listen
to tender voices,
the grass rising
for new footsteps,
the ashes embracing
a new solidity.

A brook clatters
into a stone trough
a cat returns
to a scorched doorstep.
I grow larger
become a giant,
now I see over
the shoulder of all horror.

## DEATH HOURS

I lie in a tent and listen to silence,
a sound akin to that following the closing of a fair,
shadows thicken, entangle gently,
pulsating now quietly, now faster,
at first they are ordered, then curiously confused
until they begin flickering vehemently, frantically,
as if I suddenly strode into the cacophony of a watchmaker's shop.

It dawns on me: my thoughts and incessant
calling have brought them here,
they swarm around me
each one with his final hour
for me to inherit;
gently the hours fill up the tent,
tick, tremor, flicker,
weaving the wreath of a turbulent silence.

As the night deepens
I see and recognize them:
the first willed me his unborn child,
the second a climb up Mt. Jalovec, the third postage stamps,
the fourth his vineyard, the fifth carnival masks,
the thirteenth a voyage around the world, the hundredth self-
        defense,
and the last one a boisterous tune and a grieving mother.

## HANDS

I have lived between my two hands
as between two brigands,
neither knowing
what the other did.
The left hand was crazed by the heart,
the right hand clever by its skill.
One took, the other lost,
they hid from one another,
only half-finishing everything.

Today as I ran from death
and fell and rose and fell,
scrambling among thorns and rocks,
my hands were equally bloodied.
I spread them like the sacrificial handles
of the great temple's candlestick,
that bear witness with equal fervor—
faith and unfaith burned with a single flame,
ascending hot and high.

## DUALITY

As if I suddenly stepped
from noise into silence
an opiating plain with quiet breathing
appeared in front of me,
a noble woman of regal beauty,
the ancient earth tamed long ago,
with its hearths, gardens and graves.

I closed my eyes
on the border of two worlds,
the dream-world and reality,
the happy and the unhappy lands,
and whispered:
O Antigone,
after I return from the hunt
I'll kneel in front of you
and serve you!

Broken voices replied
from the plain:
the duplicate strokes of a washer-woman on water
the duplicate horse's trot
the duplicate dog's barking
the duplicate child's scream
the duplicate tolling of bells.
My heart constricted:
it is all broken,
the world is split
in two parts
no longer able to unite.
The fruit of the world ripened,

the dark hour arrived.

A sudden surge of wind
disheveled my hair,
I plunged into the deep
grasping with urgent hands
at the sinewy tree trunk.

## PRIMEVAL MOTHER

Where are you, oblivion? Where are you, transient winds?
Everything passes but my sad punishment,
look at me revered to the highest mountain,
I am the oldest and closest to the beginning.

I no longer know to whom I call, who I beseech,
I am crazed by horror, singing from sorrow;
shouting and weeping blend into a melody
I've swung the angst of man since times immemorial.

I rock him with ineffable movements,
precipices amass in my blindness,
clear waterfalls storm through my deafness—
my story is older than darkness.

In my long ritual toga
I am the world's oldest sorrow,
torn apart by pain on the mountaintop
I cradle lost man in my arms.

## SUMMON

We remember
how we stampeded the ground,
tamed beasts,
supported the sky,
shouted to one another
solemn commands
to be able to endure in the cave
that the sun had carved
into the darkness of the universe.

We remember
broadening the cave
with our backs,
making the world moan,
heights flapping,
depths creaking,
the cardinal directions of the sky screaming;
then the hymen of the mysterious
started to bleed.

We finally remember
also the great prophecies,
we were born for miracles,
we shall walk the ocean surface,
fly the skies,
play ball with the earth,
and loose it in the dark—
then each of us will have to find
his own star.

Edvard Kocbek

## TARGET

Circle after circle,
horizon after horizon,
whirl after whirl,
always the one and the same
vertiginous whirlpool:
the torture wheel
of earth's eden,
the conspiring magic circle
of the magician's snare,
the hoop that closes
more and more,
the final ring
of my love.

Where can I flee from you,
mysterious iris of the eye?

You watch me from whirlwinds,
gulp me down with bubbling pools,
stare at me from caves and dens,
approach me in treetops and clouds,
speak to me in  the knots of silence,
gaze at me from gnarls,
point from the gun's barrel
at my exhausted heart.
I can no longer escape you,
sharp and greedy pupil—
the Aztec's and the Indian's,
the gypsy's and the Negro's--
deadly loving
Cyclop's eye.

## ALL DOORS ARE OPEN

The world is full of blood-thirsty persecutors,
but the worst persecution is
when you are not hunted,
but still act like a lost wild animal
tracked by an invisible hunter: when
you sit in your studio drinking coffee
or stretching bored in the office,
when even the fanciest cigar in your mouth
cannot relieve you from a dreadful sense of guilt
as if someone has a grip on you, making you
perspire with deadly fear, wishing, either you
didn't know who you were or could
throw yourself from the ninth floor.
This persecution is the most horrifying flight
from oneself, the most fatal capture.
Nothing helps, even though all doors are open
and all guns at your disposal, when you sit
amid black night or clear day
unable to move from the deadly fear
of an unknown, ineffable guilt.

## BECOMING UNSPEAKABLE

I am enraged, in the holy state
of exalted fury and dreadful anger,
the scream of the wounded and offended soul.
I punish myself and those in my reach
with enlightened curses,
clever insults and the hisses
of a whip. My doing is wholesome and sacred.

Suddenly I calm, become quiet,
silence unfolds inside
from an invisible power, permeates me,
and though I still talk my words are soft,
gentle, whispered, etched with a tender writing;
I've become ineffable, close to my essence,
a mysterious curtain between voices and silence.

I paused at the corner crammed with scents,
at the meeting place of women's evenings
where, from the topmost floor, fall
new fairy tales
causing the old ones' hearts to contract.
Perhaps I truly am prepared and
translucent, properly pious,
punished by a distant grace?

## WHO WILL DINE WITH ME TONIGHT?

Hunger in the voluptuous mouth,
thirst in the brain cells,
who will dine with me tonight?
My living is slower than my dying,
my whispers faster than my thoughts.
What am I to do with this precedence,
withering slowly, changing, like laurel, into leather?
My hungry self remembers how I,
many years ago on the same day,
was confronted by a gun
that transformed me into an unspeakable lover.
I perished that day, became someone else
invisible to others
who walked through me unable to recognize the miracle.
Each night, like a brother, a stranger sleeps inside me
as I grow more pensive
with an insatiable hunger for thoughtful truths.
Who will dine with me tonight?
I lost my spoon in the battle of Rog,
broke my fork on the Glamočki field,
and thrust my knife into a tree trunk
now supporting the vacation house of a gentleman,
my good appetite was left on the bark
of the memorial tree from paradise,
my hand trembles from breaking bread.
I am too full
and my hunger too small.

Edvard Kocbek

NOAH

A day is the candle amid darkness,
and the earth runs like a puppy
after its old master.
Fewer and fewer strings buzz inside me,
at times I play on one only
like a bard of the ill-fated millennium.

Every morning I have to
stir up from my sleep,
collect more memories,
catch more premonitions,
boomerangs return faster and faster,
the heap of questions is higher and higher.

Where did innocence go?
How do birds die?
What is the joy of madmen?
Who lies in the holy grave?
When will eternity end?
How much is nothing times nothing?

Leave me naked, sons!
I'll never sober up from darkness,
never consume to the bottom the wine
of sweet ignorant oblivion.
Man's eyes have lashes
and I am grateful for these veils.

## VEILED HORROR

Every time I step out on the street
I am increasingly alarmed.
I look at women's faces,
they are more and more beautiful
and pure-blooded,
but their beauty is becoming monotonous
and boring:
too many too perfect bodies
and too many seductresses exchangeable.

Where are the eyes that would
look down when they meet with mine,
where is healthy and pure modesty,
no face shows a request for
compassion, nothing that illuminates
from within,
only perfection, a soul without a soul,
a body without fire, a cold cruelty,
beautiful monsters, cosmetic terrors.

A man can no longer choose a woman
who would keep surprising him
until his last days,
people cannot choose their gracious
queen with a proper ceremonial devotion
even though they teach us in school
that no cathedral is ever finished
and no Trojan War ever ended.

## ON THE EVENING DOORSTEP

A mother to a daughter in the evening
as she prepares to go out
all beautiful and pure,
a mother to a daughter on the doorstep in the evening
tries to stop and tell her
tell her the ancient message,
a mother to a daughter on the doorstep in the evening
the ancient message that today is shut out
but her throat constricts, she is unable to utter a sentence
the one and only sentence, the saving grace
as no mother ever could,
no mother to a daughter on the doorstep in the evening
to a daughter and her progeny
that when she returns
she will be changed
bearing her own fruit
and one day these words will be stuck in her throat
and her daughter's and her daughter's daughter,
on the doorstep in the evening.

## SMELL OF A MIDNIGHT BLOSSOM

When they start their love-making in the heights
I am confused by the dangerous play of body and spirit.
When I lay my hand on my heart
the brass trumpets in my loins begin to sing.
When I pick up a mountain flower
the far-away galaxies start to tremble.
And when I open the door to blissful sexuality
the biblical tribes make their voices heard in an instant.

There is no soul without Adam's body
and no body without divine inspiration.
Nothing passionate or spoken can pass
through a needle's eye without a miracle.
What I am saying is: there is no inspiration without ecstasy.
In quarries lie seeds of white palaces,
in deserts plans for gardens with fountains.
In my dreamtime I am a lover, an illusion of a waterfall.

How can I stay calm under the thundering of echoes?
How can I soften the look of insanity?
The world is suspicious, without beginning.
Apocalyptic riders are abundant.
Light is darkening, only blindness still smolders.
The flood of insane materialism is increasing.
At nightfall I will break my silence and disappear.
Creep quietly into the mystery.

Edvard Kocbek

## UNKNOWN BELOVED

You do not know me
and I do not know you,
blue and green colors
do not tolerate each other.
The royal purple
is inclined to fresh red.
You are from an old tribe,
your whisper and blood blend,
everything about you is bitter
and anciently sweet.
We visit each other in secret
and make love
as defined by order,
with trembling fingers
we stagger off a table
and with a kiss carry one another
into one quivering mouth.
At times we blow dust off
the sea to elope into a clearer pain
and final breath.
Dressed in royal purple
with fragrant wings of hair
you fly off first
while I, short of breath,
turn into a messenger
with the message lost.

## FISHNET

Fishermen stand in an old fishing boat
thrusting, with distinctive motions,
long oars into the deep—now and now
and now and again—until the humble
man's zeal is halted
by the power of dark waters
challenging male strength.

In the keel a fishnet in heaps.
Folded in a heavy mass it tranquilly waits
to be spread above the depths.
The sky staggers quietly, the net sways
the boat with the men and their upturned reflection.
Peace reigns. In the center of a whirlpool
the old boat. Night falls.

## IT IS ALL CONNECTED

The infinite sky has collapsed many
times above me
and then picked itself up
like exhausted weather.
I came to terms with countless
images and punishments.
Plains had risen
and mountains were lowered
before I realized
it is all the same how the
earth flies and what curves I use
to lean on its walls;
speed has a familiar insanity about it
and transience is indifferent to
the gloomy drunkenness.
Fear and courage age
differently.
Prophets, though, all come
from the same desert.

## WHO AM I?

I am not
who they think I am,
and am never there
where eyes can see me.
Enemies think I am
an heir to the throne,
friends are convinced
I am a secretive deacon,
and jokers
see me rotting in the journal
of the fleet
sunk while searching for new lands.
But I kneel at noon
in the midst of a desert
writing a dictation of silence in the sand,
gnash my teeth at nightfall
in a dangerous crack
of Babylon's tower
and lie at midnight loyally
among the golden swords
of Hamlet's terrace.
At dawn, though,
I straddle the saddle of distances
behind seven times seven moonlights
and gallop to meet
a generous rose
ready to erupt.
One day the rose
will look
this arrogant century in the face
and the century will blush.

## SOLEMN BACKGROUND

For some days now I hear a rumbling voice
not unlike thunder's. The wind is quiet,
the sun slanting, the transience
unabated. The whole creation is in
trepidation. The hour of solitude,
the time of total desolation.
Still, I wish not to be alone, my rescue
is improbable without a sound background.
Therefore: whatever is about to come,
to approach, to reveal itself, let it not
tiptoe. Let it come solemn,
majestic, from the thundering distances.
And when it does, strike your drums, drummers,
clash, forces of the sky, roar
tall and virginal waterfalls!

## DEATH OF WORDS

I am unable to sleep,
a big disaster
surrounds me,
words that I have spoken
and sent out into the world
are suddenly returning weary,
ill, dreadfully anxious,
they seek a refuge from destruction,
flutter, squeal,
chirp haltingly, swarm around me
they are fleeing from triteness and oblivion,
from the glass eye of a corpse,
from a laser beam that ignores
its reflection,
the infected words
cram up in greedy haste, they
stammer, writhe in pain,
they've lost their way home,
their resting place,
they flutter above me
as I lie empty and mute in the dark.
I recognize them, tamed, wild,
gay and sad, dreamy,
frightened, big, treacherous,
miserable, playful, erotic,
heroic, pious, all motherly,
all mine, my father's, all my essence,
my recollections, my presentiments,
my prophecy, my dying.
The room is crammed with them,
they settle on objects, are unable to leave,

burden me, beseech me as they lie dying,
sobbing repeatedly:
all tree trunks desecrated
all nests destroyed
all mouths mute.
The disaster inhabits me,
there is no place I can return them to,
am unable to console them,
stretch my arm
or open my mouth,
am unable to caress the word despair or
say anything to the words solace, deliverance,
the words toy and grace are choking me,
on my eyes land those shot as they fled
man, mother, love, loyalty,
the unhappy ones I neglected or never uttered
settle on my chest
but one of them has nestled
right between my trembling lips,
never have I seen it in the lexicon.

DIVINE SEARCH

When my quiet thoughts reach for you, all that is sinful and alien falls off me. The world again becomes solemn, innocent and relaxed, like after a good deed. I leave the earth and take my playful feet to the open sea. I start wandering away from the soil where they sold the beautiful maiden, searching for her on the rocking ground. I begin casting spells, singing, luring toward myself, toying with depth, jumping from wave to wave, on clouds, through the ancient universe and mute grounds, singing the songs of the transient, knowing all the melodies and voices, ways of loving, ways of memories and prophecies, letting the wind rock my scars, climbing over the fantasy, the whole world belongs to me, only the song of the maiden eludes me, something essential is fleeing, I listen to the falling of quarters of the moon and echoes of hurricanes in Alaska, to the docile feeding of rustling Canadian forests, but I cannot seize her though I sense her, I, hostage, wanderer, wizard, and lover am seeking the maiden's song through the terrifying nothingness, roaming like the softest breeze through the organ's pipes, like grass through the spotty cow, or like weight through the clutch of time, I am all covered with corals, maiden, let nobody know where I am hiding and where I can find you, remain the knowing darkness and the blessed pain under the waterfalls of the river, in its clear flow from mill to mill.

## LEGEND

A Spanish princess
walks among us.
You do not see her,
do not hear her,
the prophecy
or the memory.
She walks erect,
of morning stature,
carrying a jug of evening
on her head.
Be still,
do not move,
the jug is full
of your eyes' dew.
She carries it erect
in these fickle times,
her balance
is astonishing,
do not frighten her,
have compassion for her,
for yourselves,
each drop
our ransom.
The princess walks safely
with tender courage.
She is through the door already,
starting up
up the stairs.

## PROMISED LAND

We have arrived and stopped.

The dead tired partisan squad collapsed on the ground and fell asleep. Only I was unable to find peace, the goal hid itself, I lost the shortest way to oblivion.

My disconsolate spirit keeps searching, roaming from darkness to light, from snow to blooming linden trees, from slopes to valleys, from streets to primal forests, through wind and silence, through moonlight and storms.

We resemble those who in ancient times made their pilgrimage through the Red Sea barefoot, on horseback, armored, with spears in their hands and fire in their eyes; with song on their lips and longing in their hearts, calloused, burdened, scarred, dusty, hunchbacked, loyal and happy they searched for the promised land. The primal weight of time, cramming, cursing, praying, draws me behind itself, pushing me from behind, going always forward, never backward.

One day I will pause on the forest edge at nightfall, the evening sun will make me squint, and I'll shelter my eyes with feverish hands and see before me a fertile clearing, green fields, a fenced orchard, and a house among the trees, with barns and a sunken bed in a depression of hay.

Then and only then will I find my peace, close my eyes, lean on my comrades, and wander into the wild like a sleep-walker on a roof, stuttering incoherently as if from a vision:

"When one finds the land, why seek the sky?"

# Lumen Books

### E. Luminata
Diamela Eltit
Translated by Ronald Christ
ISBN: 0-930829-40-9. $15.00

### The Narrow Act: Borges' Art of Allusion
Ronald Christ
ISBN: 0-930829-34-4. $15.00

### Written on a Body
Severo Sarduy
Translated by Carol Maier
ISBN: 0-930829-04-2. $8.95

### Borges in/and/on Film
Edgardo Cozarinsky
Translated by Gloria Waldman & Ronald Christ
ISBN: 0-930829-08-5. $10.95

### Space in Motion
Juan Goytisolo
Translated by Helen Lane
ISBN: 0-930829-03-4. $9.95

### Reverse Thunder, A Dramatic Poem
Diane Ackerman
ISBN: 0-930829-09-3. $7.95

### Byron and the Spoiler's Art
Paul West
ISBN: 0-930829-13-1. $12.95

### Urban Voodoo
Edgardo Cozarinsky
ISBN: 0-930829-15-8. $9.95

### Under a Mantle of Stars
Manuel Puig
Translated by Ronald Christ
ISBN: 0-930829-00-X. $10.00

### Refractions
Octavio Armand
Translated by Carol Maier
ISBN: 0-930829-21-2. $15.00


## www.lumenbooks.org

Trade and library orders to:
**Consortium Book Sales and Distrubution**
800-283-3572